THE GREAT PHILOSOPHERS

Consulting Editors
Ray Monk and Frederic Raphael

D0828159

HEIDEGGER

Jonathan Rée

ROUTLEDGE
New York

Published in 1999 by
Routledge
29 West 35th Street
New York, NY 10001

First published in 1997 by
Phoenix
A Division of the Orion Publishing Group Ltd.
Orion House
5 Upper Saint Martin's Lane
London WC2H 9EA

10 9 8 7 6 5 4 3 2 1

Library of Congress Cataloging-in-Publication Data

Rée, Jonathan, 1948–
        Heidegger / Jonathan Rée.
          p. cm.—(The great philosophers : 20)
        Includes bibliographical references.
        ISBN 0-415-92396-4 (pbk.)
        1. Heidegger, Martin, 1889–1976. Sein und Zeit.
        2. Ontology. 3. Space and time. I. Title. II. Series:
        Great Philosophers (Routledge (Firm)) : 20.
B3279.H483S446 1999
111—dc21   99-21674
                                                            CIP

CONTENTS

HEIDEGGER

History and Truth in Being and Time

INTRODUCTION

Universities often seem more like asylums for the protection of deluded academics than workshops producing real knowledge. Take a glance, for example, at this heavy bible-black volume issued in Halle in 1927: *Jahrbuch für Phänomenologie und phänomenologische Forschung*, Vol. 8. It is 800 pages long, and contains just two philosophical treatises, divided into numbered sections like insurance regulations. Unreadable, you will conclude: just another meaningless monument to academic pride and grandiosity.

Back in 1927, however, the German philosophical public leapt on the *Jahrbuch*. It was not Oskar Becker's meticulous discussion of 'Mathematical Existence' that attracted them, but the other article, even longer and more forbidding. The author was only an assistant professor at Marburg in Hessen at the time, but he already enjoyed a strange notoriety. It was said that he was not just a philosopher, but – on the contrary – a *thinker*, and that he cared nothing for the cosmopolitan elegance of the German intellectual aristocracy, preferring the gruff peasant manners he had been born to 37 years before, in the Catholic village of Messkirch, down in Baden. Instead of frequenting professorial dinner tables, he liked to stay with his wife and two young sons in the mountain hut he had built above Todtnauberg in the Black Forest a few years before. There he could ski across country, chop wood, gaze into the distance, and think. But he needed a better-paid job – ideally, a Chair at his old university in Freiburg-im-Breisgau, an easy car-journey from his hut – and he could not get promotion unless he published a substantial article. He sent off some manuscripts to the *Jahrbuch*, and so it was that *Being and Time: First Half* by Martin Heidegger made its entrance into the world.

The philosophical issue of the day was the relation between truth and history. Enlightenment faith in science and progress had been devastated by the war of 1914–18, leaving the field open to corrosive 'relativism'. Beliefs, it seemed, depended on the fickleness of history, not on some transcendently trustworthy absolute truth.

Heidegger's big argument would be that, if the concepts of historical particularity and scientific truth are clearly thought through, then the apparent conflict between them disappears: that our individual peculiarities are not a chrysalis that we leave behind in order to rise to an exalted realm of truth, but the origin and anchor of all our knowledge. It was going to be a hard lesson, however, since it ran counter to our most immediate sense of ourselves – to the dichotomy between mind and world or subjectivity and objectivity which, as well as being built into the brickwork of western philosophy, is woven into the fabric of our everyday self-understandings. The necessary task of clarification would require not only intellectual virtuosity, but a labour of self-transformation as well.

AN ONTOLOGY OF OURSELVES

At first it is a disappointment to move from these tantalizing expectations to the treatise Heidegger actually wrote. For a start, what title could be more outdated than *Being and Time*? Was Heidegger unaware that the philosophical study of being – 'ontology', in the jargon of the academy – had been definitively discredited by Kant at the end of the eighteenth century, and replaced by empirical natural science? And had no one told him that, following Einstein's special theory of relativity of 1905, the concept of time now belonged to physics rather than philosophy?

But we should take care. Philosophers often write with a canny sense of paradox, and eventually make fools of those with too little wariness about their own unclarified and unironic certitudes. Heidegger may not be about to bore us with some foolhardy new solutions to the problems or pseudo-problems of traditional ontology – philosophical equivalents to perpetual motion or squaring the circle. He may have something rather subtler up his sleeve.

Still, our hearts will sink again when we turn the page and discover a quotation in Greek – a remark addressed by the mysterious Eleatic stranger to the radiant youth Theaetetus in Plato's dialogue *The Sophist*: 'for manifestly you have long been aware of what you mean when you use the expression "being"'.[1] So it will be just another debate over the meanings of words, we sigh. Heidegger pursues the quotation: 'we, however, who used to think we understood it, have now become perplexed'.[2] Here is a twofold surprise. 'We *used to* think we understood it': but surely our certainties are meant to grow with age, not diminish? And '*now* we are perplexed': but is it not perpetual truth, rather than mounting perplexity, that is supposed to be the daughter of time?

At least we can be reassured that Heidegger is not going to lay down the law about the nature of being as such. His theme is less portentous – the 'meaning of being' – and this 'meaning', as he explains later, is not some mystery that 'stands behind being', but simply whatever sense the term may happen to have within our ordinary languages and understandings: the investigation, he says, will be anything but 'deep'.[3] And even if we end up discovering nothing positive, we can at least hope to clarify our understanding of the question we are asking, the *question of the meaning of being*.[4]

When we turn another page and start reading the Introduction ('Exposition of the question of the meaning of being'), we find Heidegger taking yet another step backwards. 'This question has today been forgotten', he writes. The question of being may have had some urgency when Plato and Aristotle wrestled it into submission in Athens long ago; but ever since that time it has been ignored or languidly dismissed as 'superfluous'.[5]

If the question has been forgotten, however, it is not because it has been censored and suppressed, but because it has been paraded in public so shamelessly that it has lost its original pungency. Like a poem or prayer that we learned by rote in childhood, the question of the meaning of being feels so dull and familiar that we never notice that we are ignorant of what it means: 'that which the ancient philosophers found continually disturbing as something obscure and hidden', Heidegger says, has declined into 'clarity and self-evidence'.[6]

It is precisely because of this distracting banality that Heidegger refuses to tell us directly what we no doubt want to know: what exactly does he mean by 'being'? How would he define it? He reminds us that it has always been one of the grand themes of western philosophy, but

4

beyond that he offers only broad hints: being is a crucial question, perhaps the mother and father of all questions; it is an issue that belongs to all of us, whether we know it or not; it is what we are ultimately talking about, whenever we talk at all; and it has been disgracefully trivialized by the very philosophical tradition that is supposed to celebrate it. This explanation of 'being' may seem exceedingly enigmatic, but Heidegger promises that if we follow him we will eventually be able to discover within ourselves not only some glimmer of its meaning, but also some understanding of why we are all inclined to dismiss the entire issue as trivial and vexatious.

Our predictable weariness about ontology rests on some quite intriguing prejudices. First, as Heidegger points out, it presumes that being must be the most universal of concepts, since it designates what all things have in common. Secondly, it assumes that being is vague and indefinable: for how could something so general have any distinctive characteristics? The third presumption is that all of us already understand being without even having to think about it: after all, any child can use the verb 'to be', and what more could we mean by an understanding of the meaning of being?

Yet these three prejudices against ontology are themselves assumptions about being. They are ontological judgements and, as Heidegger points out, they are 'rooted in ancient ontology itself'. If we examine them closely, therefore, they may disclose something about the meaning of being, and illuminate the play of recognition and forgetting that constitutes the history of ontology. If being is indeed the most universal of concepts, then 'this cannot mean that it is the one which is clearest or that it needs no further discussion'; it suggests, on the contrary, that 'it is rather the darkest of all'. And secondly, if being is truly 'indefinable', it follows that it is categorially different from the kinds of entity we interact with in everyday life; and

5

this seems to show that ontological issues (questions about being as such) cannot be approached in the same way as *ontical* ones (questions about particular entities). Thirdly, if we possess an adequate understanding of being anyway, then we must recognize that this untutored 'average kind of intelligibility' is itself a significant fact, which deserves patient and attentive analysis.[7]

Of course, we may always be mistaken about ontological issues, whether our attitude be credulous or hostile or somewhere in between. In particular, we will be constantly tempted to treat them as if they were 'ontical' – as if they concerned one entity amongst others, and could be sufficiently explained by 'telling a story' (as in a 'history of philosophy') and tracing them 'back in their origin to some other entities, as if being had the character of some possible entity'.[8] But if we are perpetually misconstruing ontological questions by offering ontical answers to them, this only confirms that they remain an issue for us. After all, we could not exist at all without some understanding of the nature of the world around us and our place in it. This understanding need not take the form of explicit ontological opinions, of course; rather it will find expression in the way we lead our lives. From the first dawning of our existence, as Heidegger puts it, we 'already live in an understanding of being'.[9] Even if we despise the whole idea of ontology, our attempts to avoid it will still bear the imprint of what repels us. And if our ways of avoiding ontology are themselves interpretations of ontology, then we must all already be our own ontologists – amateur ontologists of our own existence.

The Question and the Questioner
But what are we doing when we inquire into the question of the meaning of being? Indeed, what does it mean to ask questions at all? Heidegger offers the following brisk analysis.

Every inquiry is a seeking. Every seeking gets guided

beforehand by what is sought … Any inquiry, as an inquiry about something, has *that which is asked about*. But all inquiry about something is somehow a questioning of something. So in addition to what is asked about, an inquiry has *that which is interrogated* … Furthermore, in what is asked about there lies also *that which is to be found out by the asking*.[10]

These words may well strike us as ungainly and defiantly obscure – especially in English. Macquarrie and Robinson's translation is a classic, but it is not perfect. Indeed, no translation could possibly do justice to the sinewy style of *Being and Time*, which constantly draws on procedures of word-formation peculiar to the German language. In this instance, Heidegger is spelling out how every *Fragen*, or asking, comprises not only (a) a preliminary notion of 'what is sought', but also (b) a *Gefragte*, which is 'asked about', (c) a *Befragte*, which is 'interrogated', and (d) an *Erfragte*, which is 'to be found out'. Part of the poetry of Heidegger's analysis might be reproduced by saying that every *asking* compromises (a) its initial orientation, (b) its *asked-about*, (c) its *asked-after* and (d) its *asked-for* – except that this sounds ridiculous in English, whereas in German the effect is simple, even beautiful.

Heidegger then applies this general analysis to the question of the meaning of being. Our preliminary orientation, he says, is provided by the 'vague average understanding of being' in terms of which we 'always conduct our activities'. This initial understanding may 'fluctuate and grow dim, and border on mere acquaintance with a word', though 'its very indefiniteness is itself a positive phenomenon which needs to be clarified'. What is *asked about* is 'being', of which we know very little except that it is utterly unlike the particular entities we encounter in everyday life. What is *asked after* or 'interrogated', on the other hand, must be 'entities' of specific kinds, 'questioned as regards their being'. And finally, what is *asked for*, or 'to be found out', is the 'meaning of being' itself.[11]

But this fourfold analysis is not complete. In order to understand a question, you also need to take account of a fifth factor – *where* it is coming from, or *who* the questioner (or 'asker' – *Frager*) is. A question about the weather obviously calls for a different response when asked by a sailor, a farmer or a back-packer. So what of the question of the meaning of being in general – the vague, obscure, charming and alarming question that we all like to think we can easily answer or as easily dismiss? Who are we when we ask it? What is the essence of its *asker*?

The peculiarity of this question is that we are engaged with it all the time. Whenever we orientate ourselves in the world and make some sense of it, or fail to do so, we stand in some relation to the question of the meaning of being: our asking of it is coextensive with our existence. One might almost say that our capacity for asking it corresponds to what is usually referred to by such terms as 'human nature' or 'mind' or 'soul', except that this vocabulary is so stuffed with strange residues of mysticism and metaphysics that it might constrain or misdirect our inquiries.

The entity we are when confronted by ontological questions is simply us, as ordinary and familiar as can be. Heidegger therefore chooses the most ordinary of German words to describe it: *Dasein*. *Dasein* can often be translated as 'existence', but in *Being and Time* that term is needed to express the concept of *Existenz*, so the only feasible solution has been to create a new English word to serve as its equivalent: 'Dasein' (written without italics; plural: 'Daseins'). In practice we can often paraphrase it by using 'we' in its place, but not always. If the foreignism still makes us stumble, we should simply remind ourselves that the German word *Dasein* is as colloquial as can be. It is not a technical term, and as Daseins, we are simply entities with ontological attitude.

If our understanding of questions always presupposes some knowledge of who is asking them, it follows, as Heidegger says, that our understanding of ontological questions will require a 'proper explication' of Dasein. The explication of Dasein will not be a logical or natural-scientific analysis, however. As human beings, we can be analysed either as logical reasoners or as physical bundles of meat and bone; but as Daseins we are nothing but our understandings and misunderstandings of the world and our place in it, and our more or less clear understandings and misunderstandings of these understandings, and so on for ever and ever without end. The connotations of the word 'analysis' may seem too hard-edged, therefore, and we may well prefer 'hermeneutic of Dasein', which is Heidegger's alternative phrase for the infinitely prolific art of interpreting our interpretations of being.[12]

There would appear to be two ways of approaching the hermeneutic of Dasein: one ontological, the other ontical. The first would seek to enter into Dasein's understanding of the meaning of being and clarify it from within, whilst the second would offer an external description of the characteristics that distinguish us, as Daseins, from other kinds of entity. But as Heidegger points out, ontical description and ontological interpretation are bound to get tangled up with each other.

> Dasein is an entity which does not just occur amongst other entities. Rather it is ontically distinguished by the fact that, in its very being, that being is an *issue* for it. But in that case, this is a constitutive state of Dasein's being, and this implies that Dasein, in its being, has a relationship towards that being ... And this means further that there is some way in which Dasein understands itself in its being, and that to some degree it does so explicitly. It is peculiar to this entity that with and through its being, this being is disclosed to it. *Understanding of being is itself a definitive characteristic of Dasein's being.* Dasein is ontically distinctive in that it *is* ontological.[13]

Dasein's ontical speciality, one might say, is universal ontology. For Dasein, to exist is to ontologize. We all have 'an understanding of being', Heidegger says, even if we are not conscious of it, and even if we have never heard of ontology and are happy to stay that way. If our existence is not always explicitly ontological, it is at least 'pre-ontological'.[14]

The purpose of deliberate ontological inquiry, then, will be a 'clarification' and 'radicalization' of our 'pre-ontological understanding of being'.[15] Through clarification and radicalization our pre-ontologies will be transformed into what Heidegger called 'fundamental ontology'. The phrase has proved an unlucky one, however: it sounds like 'fundamental physics' and evokes an image of specialized professional ontologists formulating universal principles by which to judge the fumbling efforts of us ordinary amateurs. But the journey we have already made – through the analysis of questioning to the identification of Dasein as the asker of ontological questions – should have taught us that there will be no principles of ontology outside the intersecting spirals of our own understandings of the meaning of being. Fundamental ontology will be essentially reflexive, and the 'of' of the 'hermeneutic of Dasein' will have to be understood in two different directions. The hermeneutic of Dasein is also Dasein's hermeneutic: interpretation of Dasein, by Dasein, for Dasein.

Ontological analysis of Dasein – that is, our own analysis of ourselves in our existence – can also be described as 'existential'. But existential analysis comprises nothing except our interpretations of ourselves as entities that interpret and misinterpret being. If we succeed in replacing our unconsidered pre-ontologies with more fundamental ones, it will not be by uncovering structures that are already buried there, like solid rock beneath the quaking sands of our existence, but by releasing ourselves from the illusion that our existence has any foundations at all, apart from our interpretations of it. '*Fundamental ontology*', as Heidegger puts it, 'must be sought in the *existential analytic of Dasein*.'[16] Fundamental ontology will dissolve ontological foundations and reveal that our existence has no basis but itself.

These arguments are one of the main sources of the concept of 'existentialism', which became modish in the 1950s and deeply unfashionable thereafter. But it is a term that Heidegger always shunned. Like all the 'isms' used by historians of philosophy, it presumes that the classification of ontological attitudes can have the same kind of detached objectivity as the classification of botanical specimens. It overlooks the fact that, if the history of philosophy is to be reduced to a story of philosophers making choices between various 'positions', then the historian must choose some particular position in order to make a map of the others. It forgets that there can be no position about philosophy which is not also a position within it. The self-forgetful self-certainties that underpin the concept of 'existentialism', it seems, are precisely what existential analysis is meant to save us from.

Presence and the Deconstruction of Tradition
It would be easy to interpret Heidegger's shift from the ontology of being to a hermeneutic of ourselves as reproducing the traditional philosophical turn from external observation to inner intuition, from reality to ideality, from empiricism to speculation, or from classical objectivity to romantic subjectivity. But that, Heidegger argues, would be to misconstrue our existence as Dasein, and to think of ourselves ontically rather than ontologically.

> Ontically, of course, Dasein is not only close to us – even that which is closest: we *are* it, each of us, we ourselves. In spite of this, or rather for just this reason, it is ontologically that which is farthest.[17]

Ontically, our existence can perhaps be understood as an

'inner', 'ideal' and 'subjective' process; but ontologically it occurs at a distance from ourselves, strange to us even in its familiarity. (The reader may well think of Freud at this point, though Heidegger probably did not. Like ships in the night, Freud and Heidegger were converging on the same paradox: that the vivid certainties that make up our conscious sense of who we are may always – perhaps of necessity – be self-deceptions and mistakes.) It is characteristic of Dasein, Heidegger says, that 'its own specific state of being … remains concealed from it'.[18]

For Heidegger the fundamental mechanism of self-misrecognition is our sense of 'historicality'. Perhaps we can all accept that each of us is defined, at least in part, by our place in history. Very few of us are born, as the saying goes, with a silver spoon in our mouth; but nearly all of us come into possession of an infinitely richer oral inheritance a few months later, when we learn our first language – the language that gives us names and forms for articulating the significant structures of our world. But a language is self-evidently a historical entity – an ever-changing and many-layered cultural heirloom of baffling intricacy, the product of the poetic, grammatical and philosophical labours of countless previous generations. As language-users we cannot help being part of a history that always exceeds us.

But our historicality can itself be interpreted either ontically or ontologically. Ontically, we will treat it as the passive outcome of tradition, a conglomeration of ancient cultural treasures that happen to have been handed over to us from the past. For example, we may consider western philosophy as a practice that began when Parmenides first had the idea of conceptualizing the meaning of being and making it fully 'present' to consciousness. Then we can observe how the project was passed down through Plato and Aristotle to the Latin philosophy of the Roman empire and medieval Christianity, and thence to Descartes, Kant and ourselves. Within philosophy understood in this way, as Heidegger puts it, entities have always been 'grasped in their being as "presence"', and 'this means that they are understood with regard to a definite mode of time – the "*present*"'.[19]

Ontologically, however, presence is the poisoned chalice of western philosophy as well as its Holy Grail. For the traditional understanding of presence may itself be an obstacle to our understanding of the presence of tradition. We become so keen on commemorating the tradition as a monumental intellectual heritage that we actively forget the question that set it in motion: the question of the meaning of being. Inheriting a tradition is not the same as commemorating it; indeed, it is rather the opposite. You come into possession of an inheritance by taking it over and giving it a new opening on to the future, not by tagging along behind it and taking your orientation from its past.

> When tradition thus becomes master, it does so in such a way that what it 'transmits' is made so inaccessible ... that it rather becomes concealed. Tradition takes what has come down to us and delivers it over to self-evidence; it blocks our access to those primordial 'sources' from which the categories and concepts handed down to us have been in part quite genuinely drawn. Indeed it makes us forget that they have had such an origin, and makes us suppose that the necessity of going back to these sources is something which we need not even understand ... Dasein no longer understands the most elementary conditions which would alone enable it to go back to the past in a positive manner and make it productively its own.[20]

If, as the traditional metaphor suggests, our traditions are our roots, then the traditional idea of tradition uproots us from it. If we want our existence to root itself genuinely in tradition, we must look ahead, not behind:

> Any Dasein ... *is* its past, whether explicitly or not. And this is so not only in that its past is, as it were, pushing

itself along 'behind' it, and that Dasein possesses what is past as a property which ... sometimes has after-effects upon it: Dasein 'is' its past in the way of *its* own being, which, to put it roughly, 'historizes' out of its future on each occasion ... Its own past – and this always means the past of its 'generation' – is not something which *follows along after* Dasein, but something which already goes ahead of it.[21]

Within the western philosophical tradition, ontology has been boxed in by the notion of presence, and as a result the very notion of tradition has been deformed. We cannot do justice to the tradition without doing violence to the past-oriented view of history that it has bequeathed to us. We must therefore attempt what Heidegger calls a *Destruktion der Geschichte der Ontologie*: 'destroying the history of ontology' in the classic translation, though we might prefer to say 'de-structuring' or – to borrow Jacques Derrida's coinage – *deconstruction*. Destroying or deconstructing the history of ontology is not a matter of annihilating the philosophy of the past, but of retrieving it as a philosophy to come – a future philosophy that will look forward to its past and revel in its endless novelty.

At the end of the Introduction to *Being and Time*, Heidegger explains that he has set himself a twofold task, which will demand a treatise divided into two parts. Part One will pursue the analysis of Dasein in the light of the paradox that what is ontically most familiar to us is ontologically most strange. (Specifically, it will show, in three systematic divisions, that whenever we try to understand ourselves, we automatically reach for categories that are not really applicable to us as questioners, but only to ordinary 'worldless' items that we encounter in our world.)[22] And Part Two will plot the ins and outs of traditional ontology by means of a kind of inverted history of philosophy. (There will be one division each on Aristotle, Descartes and Kant, but in reverse chronological order, so as to show how

– by giving a false value to 'presence' – the traditional understanding of the Great Philosophers, including their own self-understanding, perpetuates a misunderstanding of the tradition to which they belong.)[23] We should be prepared, therefore, for an uncomfortable journey – a disconcerting voyage through paradox and inversion, in which we shall always be trying to understand ourselves in our own self-understanding, despite its inherent tendency to misunderstand us.

EVERYDAYNESS, UNDERSTANDING AND THE HISTORY OF TRUTH

'We are ourselves the entities to be analysed.'[24] That is how *Being and Time* opens, when at last it gets under way; and for a while we will be engaged in an unexpectedly pleasant and relaxing cruise around the familiar structures of our 'being-in-the-world' in its 'average everydayness'.[25] We all know, as Heidegger points out, that we need some general sense of our environment and where we are in it before we can understand anything else. As infants clinging to our mothers, or drivers planning a cross-country route, or scientists conducting an experiment, we are always 'already in a world'.[26] The 'spatiality' of Dasein, as Heidegger calls it, is a finite human situation comprising qualitatively differentiated places, rather than a homogeneous geometrical space pervading an infinite cosmos. Places lie above or below us, to our left or right, on our path or off it, and they are defined by the various activities or amenities – cooking or sleeping, toothbrush or telephone – that are 'ready-to-hand' (*zuhanden*) within them. 'What we encounter as closest to us', Heidegger says, 'is the room; and we encounter it not as something "between four walls" in a geometrical spatial sense, but as equipment for residing.'[27] Even the sun functions for us as a piece of ready-to-hand 'equipment':

> The sun, whose light and warmth are in everyday use, has its own places – sunrise, midday, sunset, midnight … Here we have something which is ready-to-hand with uniform constancy, although it keeps changing … The house has its sunny side and its shady side; the way it is divided up into 'rooms' is orientated towards these, and so is the 'arrangement' within them, according to their character as equipment. Churches and graves, for

instance, are laid out according to the rising and the setting of the sun – the regions of life and death.[28]

The system of equipment with which we surround ourselves may be rough and ready, but in its own terms it is, as Heidegger observes, perfectly clear and precise. When we say that it is 'half an hour to the house', or 'a stone's throw' or 'as long as it takes to smoke a pipe', we are not attempting to 'measure off a stretch of space' for the benefit of some 'eternal observer exempt from Dasein'. Our descriptions may be 'imprecise and variable if we try to compute them', but 'in the everydayness of Dasein they have their own definiteness which is thoroughly intelligible'.[29]

The familiar human world is as close to us as could be, but also curiously inconspicuous. There is nothing harder than 'just looking' at the geometry of a room in which you live, for instance, or inspecting your hands as if they were hunks of meat on a butcher's bench. Rooms, hands, toothbrushes and telephones show their readiness-to-hand precisely by *not* attracting our attention. It is only when they break or stop working that we notice them as physical objects in their own right, characterized no longer by 'readiness' but by what Heidegger calls 'presence-at-hand' (*Vorhandenheit*) – that is to say, the kind of unbiddable neutral objectivity sought after by the natural sciences.[30]

The suggestion that everyday practical readiness-to-hand has priority over scientific and theoretical presence-at-hand has proved congenial to 'pragmatist' followers of William James or the later Wittgenstein, and it accords well with humanist, feminist and deep-ecological criticism of 'scientism'. But the resemblances, though real, are also misleading. In expounding the distinction between readiness and presence-at-hand, Heidegger was trying to explicate Dasein's own understanding of its everyday being-in-the-world, rather than proposing a fresh theory of his own. Moreover, having shown how Dasein accords a certain priority to readiness, Heidegger immediately identified an equal and opposite force impelling it to give precedence to presence-at-hand – a kind of destiny that turns us against the human world and towards abstract knowledge, against the warm and many-coloured 'entities which we proximally encounter' in favour of the chilly grey-on-grey of impersonal theory. Heidegger was not taking sides, but merely showing how the supposed conflict between practical readiness and theoretical presence takes shape within our ontologizing, and how – whether well founded or not – it is certainly 'not accidental'.[31]

According to Heidegger, the effects of the dispute between practice and theory can be discovered writ large throughout the traditions of western philosophy. The ancient Greeks, for instance, had an excellent word for items of everyday equipment: they called them *pragmata*, meaning 'that which one has to do with in one's concernful dealings or *praxis*'.[32] But when they came to philosophize, they attributed supreme reality not to *pragmata* but to other-worldly objects beyond our reach. Their theoreticist interpretation of being was subsequently translated into Latin and became, first, the scholastic 'onto-theology' of the middle ages, and then the science-oriented 'metaphysics' of Descartes, which 'narrowed down the question of the world to that of things of nature', in particular to those aspects of reality that can be represented by 'clear and distinct' ideas: in other words, the concepts and metrics of mathematical physics.[33] The essential tendency of Cartesianism was to downgrade the practical human world by treating it as an obscure confusion due to the projection of 'subjective values' on to an indifferent world of 'objective facts'.[34]

> The kind of being which belongs to entities within-the-world is something which they themselves might have been permitted to present; but Descartes does not let them do so. Instead he prescribes for the world its 'real' being, as it were, on the basis of ... an idea in which being is equated with constant presence-at-hand.[35]

Despite its violence, however, Cartesianism is hard to resist. It is 'not an oversight which it would be simple to correct', as Heidegger puts it. It is more than the musing of a lonely French meditator, and it is not mere error, if indeed it is error at all. And it is also more than just the court philosophy of modernity, or a culmination of the ontological tradition of ancient Greece; for it is rooted in our existence, and 'grounded in a kind of being which belongs essentially to Dasein itself'.[36]

Once we have grasped how our understanding and misunderstanding of the world are structured by the distinction between readiness and presence-at-hand, we may recall that the world also contains entities of a third kind, namely ourselves. And we do not need to be very experienced in philosophical rumination to realize that when we pursue the question of our own nature we are liable to end up on rather marshy ground. 'I am myself', we may say, half-consciously imagining that the world contains entities called 'selves' (or 'personalities' or 'identities'), one of which happens to be our own. In that case, however, we will be taking ourselves to be distinct from our selves, which is paradoxical, to say the least.

We may never have heard of Descartes, but we seem to fall very easily into the habits of ontologizing associated with his name – 'reifying' ourselves, or treating the 'I' as if it were a 'thing' at large in the world, though a thing of a rather peculiar kind: soul, perhaps, or spirit, consciousness, person, subject, or mind – in short, a ghost somehow imprisoned in the machine of our body.[37] We keep returning to the idea that the foundation of our knowledge is 'the givenness of the "I"'.[38] We construe our perceptions of the world as if they were a matter of 'returning with one's booty to the "cabinet" of consciousness after one has gone out and grasped it'.[39] Similarly, we assume that our knowledge of others depends on jumping, by means of 'empathy' or 'projection', out of our own self-enclosed subjectivity and hoping to land in that of someone else.[40]

But we will not be able to sustain this proto-Cartesian egocentrism for ever. We need only glance at 'the stock of phenomena belonging to everyday Dasein' to become uneasy about treating selfhood as if it were an isolated private inner space. We know perfectly well that consciousness does not start with self-consciousness: we perceive things out in the world, not inside our heads, and when we relate to other people we encounter them directly, without first having to 'project' a 'self' into them. Indeed, it is common knowledge that self-consciousness takes us away from ourselves: we cannot even speak normally or walk naturally across a room when we are self-conscious about it.

> Perhaps when Dasein addresses itself in the way which is closest to itself, it always says 'I am this entity', and in the long run says this loudest when it is 'not' this entity. Dasein is in each case mine, and this is its constitution; but what if this should be the very reason why, proximally and for the most part, Dasein *is not itself*. What if the aforementioned approach, starting with the givenness of the 'I' to Dasein itself, and with a rather patent self-interpretation of Dasein, should lead the existential analytic, as it were, into a pitfall?[41]

It is clear, for instance, that our existence in the everyday world of ready-to-hand equipment is always social. It occurs essentially 'with others', rather than in the 'isolated "I"' of our Cartesian imaginations.[42]

> When, for example, we walk along the edge of a field but 'outside it', the field shows itself as belonging to such and such a person, and decently kept up by him; the book we have used was bought at so-and-so's shop and given by such-and-such a person, and so forth.[43]

Everyday existence always takes place in a world shared with others – not others as opposed to us, but others like us

20

and with us. We are never Dasein on our own, but always 'Dasein-with' (*Mitdasein*); our being is 'being-with' (*Mitsein*), and, despite the gravitational pull of our spontaneous Cartesianism, even self-knowledge is 'grounded in being-with'.[44] Thus those who work together in a common cause do not obstruct each other's existence but enhance it:

> When they devote themselves to the same affair in common ... they thus become *authentically* bound together, and this makes possible the right kind of objectivity (*Sachlichkeit*), which frees the other in his freedom for himself.

In the same way, we may cherish someone 'not in order to take away his "care" but rather to give it back to him authentically as such for the first time' – and that, presumably, is the essence of genuine teaching and true friendship.[45] 'The world of Dasein', as Heidegger puts it, 'is a with-world (*Mitwelt*).'[46]

Inauthenticity and the They-self

It may be one of the best-known phrases in English poetry, but 'I wandered lonely as a cloud' is also one of the strangest. No one can really be as lonely as a cloud – not even Descartes, try as he might to reify his meditative soul. Indeed, the cloud itself cannot be that lonely: loneliness can only afflict an entity whose being is essentially being-with. In the same way, treating others 'as if they did not exist' is an insult only if they have first been recognized as 'existing'. Loneliness and rudeness, in short, are not negations of being-with, but perverse or distressed forms of it.[47]

Heidegger will now dwell at some length on how authentic being-with-others degenerates into mere 'being-among-one-another', and thus into inauthenticity (*Uneigentlichkeit*). Inauthenticity is what happens when we do not 'own' ourselves – when we overlook the peculiarity of our existence as interpreters of the world, that is to say as Daseins, and treat ourselves as if we were just another of the ready-to-hand or present-at-hand entities that we have come across in the course of our experience. Inauthenticity arises, in particular, when we understand ourselves as Cartesian selves, and live our lives in terms of what Jean-Jacques Rousseau would call *amour propre*, constantly looking over our shoulders and comparing our 'selves' with those of others. We become obsessed with being ahead or behind, or grander or pettier, with whether we are as stylish as others, or as clever and experienced, or as pretty and young. In our anxiety to differentiate ourselves from others, however, we become dependent on them – not on anyone in particular, but on the other in general, or what Heidegger called *das Man*, or *the 'they'*. (The German word *Man* corresponds to the pronoun 'one' – as in 'a room of one's own' – but the phrase *the 'one'* sounds so strange in English that we have to make do with *the 'they'*.) Under the sway of the 'they', we descend from 'being-with' into 'being-among-one-another'.

> We take pleasure as *they* take pleasure; we read, see, and judge about literature and art as *they* see and judge; likewise we shrink back from the 'great mass' as *they* shrink back … Everyone is the other, and no one is himself. The *'they'*, which supplies the answer to the *'who'* of everyday Dasein, is the *'nobody'* to whom every Dasein has already surrendered itself in being-among-one-another.[48]

The 'they', Heidegger explains, teaches us to pass everything off as 'familiar and accessible to everyone', thereby making sure that 'everything gets obscured'.[49]

The fifteen pages that Heidegger devoted to the flourishing of 'inauthenticity' under the 'dictatorship of the "they"'[50] are probably the best known in the whole of *Being and Time*, but perhaps the least understood as well. As usual, the language of Heidegger's analysis is drawn from ordinary life; but on this occasion it has a shrill tone of moralistic indignation. The 'they-self' (*das Man-selbst*) is described in terms of its threefold 'falling' (*Verfallen*) into inauthenticity. As the they-self, we have always fallen into 'idle talk': we 'scribble' and 'gossip', and 'pass the word along', not in order to say things about the world, but merely to fend off silence and maintain 'communication' for communication's sake. In idle talk, we

> do not so much understand the entities which are talked about; we already are listening only to what is said-in-the-talk as such. What is said-in-the-talk gets understood; but what the talk is about is understood only approximately and superficially.[51]

The corruption of discourse means that genuine questioning gets overwhelmed by our nervous desire to be well informed and up-to-date about what is generally believed to be going on – in other words, it declines into 'curiosity', the second form of inauthenticity.

> Curiosity is characterised by a specific way of *not tarrying* alongside what is closest ... In not tarrying, curiosity is concerned with the constant possibility of *distraction* ... It concerns itself with a kind of knowing, but just in order to have known.[52]

Thanks to idle talk and curiosity, we learn to occupy ourselves with issues about which 'anyone can say anything'. We inoculate ourselves against surprises, grow indifferent to the distinctions between proof and suspicion or truth and belief, and descend into the third form of inauthenticity, which Heidegger calls 'ambiguity'.

> Everything looks as if it were genuinely understood, genuinely taken hold of, genuinely spoken, though at bottom it is not; or else it does not look so, and yet at bottom it is ... Idle talk and curiosity take care in their ambiguity to ensure that what is genuinely and newly created is out of date as soon as it emerges before the public ... Talking about things ahead of the game and

making surmises about them curiously, gets passed off as what is really happening.[53]

To make matters still worse, we embrace our they-self existence with enthusiasm, congratulating ourselves on the maturity of our self-knowledge, the fullness of our lives, and the richness of our culture. Our 'downward plunge' is concealed from us, as Heidegger says, and even 'gets interpreted as a way of "ascending" and "living concretely"'.[54]

These bilious evocations of the pompous triviality of everydayness have obvious affinities with the celebrated denunciations of industrialism to be found in Ruskin, D. H. Lawrence and F. R. Leavis, with the romantic anti-capitalism of Thoreau or William Morris, with Marx's critique of the 'fetishism of commodities', or with conservative laments about the erosion of true community in 'modernity'. Heidegger, however, protested that his analyses were 'far removed from any moralizing critique' – they did not, he claimed, 'express any negative evaluation' or imply 'a "fall" from a purer and higher "primal status"'.[55] Indeed, he pointed out that generalized denunciations of the 'great mass' of humanity are themselves the work of the they-self.[56] Falling into idle talk, curiosity and ambiguity was a feature of 'primitive societies' and of ancient Greece, as much as of modern Europe. Inauthenticity was not an ethical defect of the weak-willed, but a necessary structure of our existence as self-interpreting entities who cannot help interpreting ourselves inappropriately: that is to say, in terms of the world.

Our inherent 'capacity for delusion', Heidegger says, has an 'existentially positive character'. We are constantly in a state of 'falling' because as long as we live we can never achieve stable equilibrium, let alone a state of rest.[57] At best, we are held in suspense between opposed but incommensurable movements. The first movement is simply 'how we are' at any moment. Whether serene or indignant, elated or sad, we are always 'thrown' into some mood or other.[58] And any mood is bound to be delusive in some connections but revealing in others. If we are tormented by jealousy or immobilized by grief, then the 'abundance of things which can be discovered by simply characterizing them' will become inaccessible to us, and we will be incapacitated for purely factual scientific inquiry. On the other hand, there are some matters that we cannot understand unless we are upset: 'it is precisely when we see the "world" unsteadily and fitfully', Heidegger says, 'that the ready-to-hand shows itself in its specific worldhood, which is never the same from day to day'.[59]

But our 'thrownness' – the movement that has always landed us, willy nilly, in some mood that we cannot fully comprehend – is countered by a movement in which we 'throw' ourselves outwards, becoming 'more' than we already are as we attempt to understand the world.[60] Every understanding is projected from a mood we have been thrown into, and every mood throws out an understanding that it projects into the world: we exist, essentially, as 'thrown projection'.[61]

The two movements of our existence – 'thrown' mood and 'projective' understanding – can never be synthesized or harmonized or mutually calibrated. In our attempts at self-understanding, we will always be neglecting one or other of them. Projecting out of thrownness and thrown into projection, 'Dasein has in every case already gone astray and failed to recognise itself.'[62]

This does not mean that self-knowledge cannot hope to become rigorous and even scientific; only that it can 'never be as independent of the standpoint of the observer as our knowledge of nature is supposed to be'. Self-understanding never starts work on a new canvas: it is always in progress, and never reaches completion. We cannot understand ourselves, or see through our own self-misunderstandings and correct them, except in terms of our own understand ing. We have no choice but to argue in a circle. 'What is decisive', Heidegger says, 'is not to come out of the circle but to come into it in the right way.'[63]

Anxiety and Truth in the Clearing of Care

When we think of 'authentic existence', the picture that at first suggests itself is of a rugged and defiant individual who refuses to be smoothed out by convention or swept along by the crowd. But it should not take us long to see that this image has that peculiar combination of 'sham clarity' and profound muddle typical of the they-self: it represents, in fact, an inauthentic interpretation of authenticity.[64] It draws on the myth of a prelapsarian 'self-point', or 'isolated "I"', or 'idealised absolute subject' – so many 'residues of Christian theology', as Heidegger says, 'which have not as yet been radically extruded'.[65] Deep down, however, we know that we do not exist in the same thing-like way as clouds or clocks. We are not 'worldless' items within the world, but sites at which the world is revealed – disclosed to each of us according to our idiosyncratic spins and angles of interpretation. We are essentially 'worlded': in the world rather than of it. '*Dasein is its disclosedness*', as Heidegger puts it. '*As* being-in-the-world it is cleared in itself ... in such a way that it *is* itself the clearing (*die Lichtung*).'[66] We are not like a sturdy oak in the great forest of being, but an aimless winding path or an open glade.

The peculiarities of existence as the clearing of being can all be captured, Heidegger suggests, by a single word: 'care' (*Sorge*). The world can be defined as what we care for, and we can be defined as what cares for the world. But as care we are riven in two, in a way that recalls the unsynthesizable movements of 'thrown projection': we are divided, one might say, between *having care* (bearing down on us as a burden from the past) and *taking care* (over possibilities that we project into the future). As care, we are not a steady object within the world, but an extended network of attentiveness to it. Contrary to what the they-self would

26

imagine, we cannot approach authenticity by trying to absent ourselves from the world, but only by identifying ourselves scrupulously with the threads of care that bind it together. Care reveals our existence as always *'ahead-of-itself-in-already-being-in-a-world'*.[67]

'This above all: to thine own self be true', says Polonius to Laertes. It may seem an uncharacteristically authentic remark to emerge from the lips of Hamlet's 'foolish prating knave', but in fact it is a typical counsel of the they-self. For Polonius is advising his son to cleave to a 'self' that supposedly lurks within him like a magic jewel: he wants him to be *sincere* rather than authentic. Authenticity, threading its way through the world with lucid care, would destroy the Polonian illusion of an 'own self'. The emblem of authenticity is not a clenched fist but an open hand.

Your existence as an individual is not a given fact of nature; rather you are 'individualized' in your existence, either authentically or inauthentically. In your average everydayness, you will have identified with the listless isolation of the they-self; but you can always be brought round to yourself again, not as a mythical concentrated 'self-point', but as the dispersed clearing and disclosedness that you authentically are. For example, you may be taken aback by a work of art: and instead of being carried away from the world, as classical aesthetics might lead you to expect, you find yourself attached to it more decisively then ever. The same may happen if you are dumbfounded by the beauty of a landscape or a human body. Within *Being and Time*, however, it is anxiety (*Angst*) that provides the royal road to authenticity. Anxiety, Heidegger argues, is a kind of ontological queasiness that creeps up on you whenever you come close to understanding the inherent instability of your existence. It is like fear, only worse: a bottomless apprehensiveness that you can never comprehend.

That in the face of which one has anxiety is characterised by the fact that what threatens is *nowhere*. Anxiety 'does not know' what that in the face of which it is anxious is. ... That which threatens cannot bring itself close from a definite direction within what is close by; it is already 'there', and yet nowhere; it is so close that it is oppressive and stifles one's breath, and yet it is nowhere.[68]

The indefiniteness of anxiety is not due to imperceptiveness, however: it gives perfect expression to the quality of authentic existence, with its strangely familiar combination of the utterly familiar with the totally strange – in short, its uncanniness (*Unheimlichkeit*).

In anxiety one feels '*uncanny*'. Here the peculiar indefiniteness of that which Dasein finds itself alongside in anxiety, comes proximally to expression ... As Dasein falls, anxiety brings it back from its absorption in the 'world'. Everyday familiarity collapses. Dasein has been individualized, but individualized *as* being-in-the-world.[69]

Yet your individuality as being-in-the-world has nothing in common with the individualism of the they-self:

Anxiety individualizes Dasein and thus discloses it as '*solus ipse*' [itself alone]. But this existential 'solipsism' is so far from the displacement of putting an isolated subject-thing into the innocuous emptiness of a world-less occurring, that in an extreme sense what it does is precisely to bring Dasein face to face with its world as world, and thus bring it face to face with itself as being-in-the-world.[70]

Existential solipsism is the exact opposite of solipsism in the classical sense: not a timid retreat from the world, but a bold discovery and reappropriation of it.

On the other hand, Heidegger's account of anxiety and authenticity seems to lend itself to formulation as an old-fashioned moral fable: a story of how Dasein when young was nothing but natural disclosedness in the with-world; how it was then seduced and corrupted by the blandishments of inauthenticity; and how it at last succumbed to anxiety, repented, and came back home to authentic selfhood. But this kind of narrativization destroys Heidegger's argument, since disclosedness, the they-self and authentic individualization are not alternative ways of life, like that of the fool, the sinner and the saint, but mutually dependent forms of self-interpretation, as inseparable and indistinguishable as the opposite sides of a Möbius strip.

Different forms of self-understanding, moreover, correspond to different interpretations of philosophical tradition. The conventional view of it, codified in textbooks since the middle of the nineteenth century, is centred on the 'problem of knowledge'. The issue is supposed to have come to light when Descartes refuted 'naive realism' by showing that our perceptions often mislead us, which suggested that we might never know anything except the interior fixtures and furnishings of our own minds.[71] This, so the story goes, left philosophy with the task of 'refuting the sceptic', which divided philosophers into 'realists' (like Descartes), who believed they could prove the existence of an 'external world', and 'idealists' (like Berkeley) who did not.[72] At the end of the eighteenth century, however, Kant denounced this dispute as 'a scandal of philosophy and of human reason in general' and brokered a kind of compromise between the two sects.[73]

Heidegger has no difficulty in showing that this interpretation of the history of philosophy is itself founded on a philosophical prejudice – the view that knowledge must start from the 'inner experience' of an 'isolated subject'.[74]

> If one were to see the whole distinction between the 'inside' and the 'outside' and the whole connection between them which Kant's proof presupposes, and if one were to have an ontological conception of what has been presupposed in this presupposition, then the possibility of holding that a proof of the 'existence of

things outside me' is a necessary one which has yet to be given, would collapse.

The 'scandal of philosophy' is not that this proof has yet to be given, but that *such proofs are expected and attempted again and again.*[75]

The 'scandal', in other words, is that philosophy is expected to bend its efforts to 'refuting the sceptic' – a task which is not only intellectually boring but existentially incoherent. Who, after all, is this 'sceptic' supposed to be? 'The question of whether there is a world at all and whether its being can be proved, makes no sense if it is raised by *Dasein* as being-in-the-world; and who else would raise it?'[76] The problem can be taken seriously only as long as 'the kind of being of the entity which does the proving and makes requests for proofs has *not been made definite enough*'. It assumes, in other words, that Dasein is 'a subject which is proximally *worldless* or unsure of its world, and which must, at bottom, first assure itself of a world'.[77] We cannot even say that Dasein 'presupposes' the existence of the world, since 'with such presuppositions, Dasein always comes "too late"; … it is, *as an entity*, already in a world'.[78] And if a real sceptic does exist, then 'he does *not* even *need* to be refuted', since 'in so far as he *is*, and has understood himself in this being, he has obliterated Dasein in the desperation of suicide; and in doing so, he has also obliterated truth'.[79]

The histories of philosophy inform us that the 'problem of truth' goes back to Aristotle, who defined truth as a 'correspondence' between two kinds of entity: judgements on the one hand and objects on the other.[80] But this problem too is existentially incoherent. We could not grasp the idea of a correspondence between judgements and objects unless we already had some more fundamental understanding of truth, and a rudimentary appreciation of its intrinsic superiority to falsehood. As beings-in-the-world, we must always already exist 'both in the truth and in untruth'.[81] Yet our precious original understanding of truth, instead of being treasured and lovingly nurtured by the philosophical tradition, seems to have been brutally ignored ever since the time of 'the Greeks', and 'the concealment implicit in their ontology'.

> Truth as disclosedness and as being-towards uncovered entities – a being which itself uncovers – has become truth as agreement between things which are present-at-hand within-the-world.

The 'traditional conception of truth', Heidegger concludes, is 'ontologically derivative'. It goes back to the moment when Greek philosophers tried to remove truth and falsehood from the world and 'switched' them for inert logical properties of abstract intellectual conjectures.[82]

But Heidegger does not recommend that we scrap the dogged ratiocinations of 'the "good" old tradition' and return to a kind of sentimental subjectivistic irrationalism. That, as he remarks, would be a 'dubious gain'.[83] But it is not the choice we face. Everything can be interpreted either authentically or inauthentically, and that includes not only Dasein but also the philosophical tradition. As traditionally understood, the classics of philosophy are guided by existentially incoherent questions that reduce words like 'world' and 'truth' to mere shadows of themselves, 'levelling them off to that unintelligibility which functions in turn as a source of pseudo-problems'. If we reinterpret them in the light of authentic problems, however, they will come back into their own, and we will discover that 'the *force of the most elemental words* in which Dasein expresses itself ' is 'simultaneously alive' within them.[84]

The existential analysis of truth will reveal that traditional philosophy is rather more intelligent than philosophical tradition makes it out to be. If the analysis has any novelty, it will not be because it is unprecedented, but because it reaches authentically to the past, responding freshly to 'what was primordially surmised in the *oldest* tradition of ancient philosophy'. Authentic philosophizing

31

does not require us to have *'shaken off* the tradition', but rather to have made it authentically our own, and *'appropriated* it primordially'.[85]

The classics of philosophy all bear witness to a certain affinity between being and truth. 'In ontological problematics,' as Heidegger says, *'being* and *truth* have, from time immemorial, been brought together if not entirely identified.'[86] But whilst the association is familiar, it is also surprising, since 'truth' is clearly a property of our judgements, and therefore dependent on the historical conventions that give our words their meanings, whereas 'being' has traditionally been exalted above contingency, and accorded an objective existence quite independent of us. By associating being with truth, therefore, philosophy seems to have been whispering seditiously against its own official doctrine of absolute objectivity.

But maybe being has nothing to fear from its relationship with truth. The achievements of science need not be endangered when objectivity is interpreted in terms of Dasein's existence as disclosedness; indeed, if Heidegger is right, they will be 'rescued' by such an interpretation.[87]

> Dasein, as constituted by disclosedness, is essentially in the truth. Disclosedness is a kind of being which is essential to Dasein. *'There is'* truth only in so far as Dasein *is and so long as Dasein is.* Entities are uncovered only *when* Dasein *is*; and only as long as Dasein *is*, are they disclosed. Newton's laws, the principles of contradiction, any truth whatever – these are true only as long as Dasein *is*. Before there was any Dasein, there was no truth; nor will there be any after Dasein is no more. For in such a case truth as disclosedness, uncovering, and uncoveredness, *cannot* be. Before Newton's laws were discovered, they were not 'true'; it does not follow that they were false, or even that they would become false if ontically no discoveredness were any longer possible.

Just as little does this 'restriction' imply that the being-true of 'truths' has in any way been diminished.

To say that before Newton his laws were neither true nor false, cannot signify that before him there were no such entities as have been uncovered and pointed out by those laws. Through Newton the laws became true; and with them, entities became accessible in themselves to Dasein. Once entities have been uncovered, they show themselves precisely as entities which beforehand already were. Such uncovering is the kind of being which belongs to 'truth'.[88]

It is only because Newton's laws are projections of Dasein's historically situated existence that they can reveal to us a permanent aspect of nature as it really is. *'All truth is relative to Dasein's being'*, Heidegger says: otherwise science would be beyond us. Science is undoubtedly historical; but history is no enemy to truth.

CONSCIENCE, TIME AND THE
TRUTH OF HISTORY

If Division One of *Being and Time* has been successful, it will have persuaded us that our existence is nothing but our being-in-the-world, whether in falsehood or in truth. We will have accepted that within this world there are items of everyday 'equipment' which we relate to in a practical human way, as well as present-at-hand 'things of nature' which we can treat as objects of impersonal theory. We will also have acknowledged our inherent tendency to interpret ourselves 'in terms of the world', and thus to falsify our existence and entangle ourselves in the inauthenticity of the they-self. Furthermore, we will have noticed that traditional philosophy as a whole can be seen as conspiring to underwrite our inauthenticity.

But we have also been shown some paths that lead away from inauthenticity, demonstrating that we are not in fact self-enclosed and self-centered Cartesian selves, but receptive openings on to the world. We have been reminded of 'a potentiality-for-hearing which is genuine, and a being-with-one-another which is transparent', and thus granted a certain intimation of authentic selfhood.[89]

Authenticity can never be a comfortable condition, however. It means understanding ourselves existentially, and making this understanding our own; but that entails accepting that we are no more than shifting networks of interpretations, without any internal 'essence' to hold our existence together, and this prospect may not please us. We would prefer to be something rather more substantial, so we flee from our authentic self again and construe ourselves as items of equipment or things of nature rather than mere beings-in-the-world.[90]

At the same time, our tendency to avoid the truth about

ourselves and take refuge in inauthenticity is more than just a mistake – a foolish error that we might hope to correct and grow out of; indeed it is a genuine part of authentic existence. Inauthentic and authentic selfhood are not like a forged banknote as opposed to a genuine one, or ersatz coffee compared to the real thing. Inauthenticity is nothing but authenticity misunderstood, and authenticity is the understanding of inauthenticity. Authenticity is 'not something which floats above falling everydayness', Heidegger says, but simply 'a modified way in which such everydayness is seized upon'.[91] It haunts us as we surrender ourselves to the protection of the they, like a difficult truth that we always ignore but can never quite forget. 'Common sense misunderstands understanding', as Heidegger puts it.[92] It does so of necessity, but with an always uneasy conscience.

Conscience is itself a prime example of a form of understanding that common sense misunderstands. We imagine it as a kind of voice that murmurs to us with uncannily accurate reproaches about our most secret faults. Then, with the encouragement of traditional philosophy and Christian theology, we go on to interpret it as a call from a transcendent power that has unlimited access to our secrets, and we envisage some terrible checklist in which all our faults, however slight, will be mercilessly and irrevocably ticked off. But even as we articulate this image, something – our conscience, perhaps – will tell us that our interpretation has gone astray. We know that the voice in which our conscience calls to us is not that of an outside agency, noisy and importunate. The voice of conscience is our own voice, a still and patient potentiality whose very silence, as Heidegger puts it, can remind us of 'the possibility of another kind of hearing'.[93] Conscience is our own authentic self summoning itself from out of the they-self:

When the they-self is appealed to, it gets called to the

35

self. But it does not get called to that self which can become for itself an 'object' on which to pass judgment, nor to that self which inertly dissects its 'inner life' with fussy curiosity, nor to that self which one has in mind when one gazes 'analytically' at psychical conditions and what lies behind them. The appeal to the self in the they-self does not force it inwards upon itself, so that it can close itself off from the 'external world'. The call passes over everything like this and disperses it, so as to appeal solely to that self which, notwithstanding, is in no other way than being-in-the-world.[94]

Conscience is not a spiritual hygienist, instructing us to wash off the grime of the world and hold ourselves aloof from it; it is, on the contrary, a reminder of the fact that we are inextricably tied to the world by threads of care. It recalls us to our existence as thrown projection, and renews our recognition that it is impossible to have 'power over one's ownmost being from the ground up'.[95] That is why an authentic conscience is always a 'guilty' one: to have a 'good conscience' is to have no conscience at all. Moreover, conscience is ontological before it is ethical: it is 'the call of care', revealing to us the chronic raggedness, disunity and incompletion of our being-in-the-world.[96]

Death and the Time of Existence
There is an obvious sense, however, in which each of us will eventually reach completion, whether we like it or not. We do not live for ever, after all; and the sum total of our existence could be defined as what will be subtracted from the world by our death. But that only intensifies the problem, for how could we ever be in a position to conceptualize this totality? As long as we live, we anticipate the future: we are essentially inhabited by what Heidegger calls 'a constant "lack of totality"', a perpetual overhang of unfinished business. It is not only our present existence but also this reaching forwards that eventually 'finds an end

36

with death'.[97] It will always be both too early and too late to grasp our existence as a whole.

You might imagine that you could totalize your existence analogically, by observing the deaths of others and applying what you learn to your own case. But the analogy will always let you down at the crucial point. The death of someone else is the end of their world, not yours; it occurs in the midst of your world, not theirs; and it will be remembered by you, not by them. When we mourn, as Heidegger points out, it is because 'the deceased has abandoned our "*world*" and left it behind'. It is always '*in terms of that world*' that we grieve.[98]

Alternatively, you might try to think of a life as reaching 'fulfilment', rather like a fruit that swells to mellow perfection and then falls plumply to the ground. But that comparison will not help you either.

> With ripeness, the fruit *fulfils* itself. But is the death at which Dasein arrives, a fulfilment in this sense? With its death, Dasein has 'fulfilled its course'. But in doing so, has it necessarily exhausted its specific possibilities? Rather, are not these precisely what gets away from Dasein? Even 'unfulfilled' Dasein ends. On the other hand, so little is it the case that Dasein comes to its ripeness only with death, that Dasein may well have passed its ripeness before the end. For the most part, Dasein ends in unfulfilment, or else by having disintegrated and been used up.[99]

You will always be too young or too old to die.

The only way you can ever understand the significance of the entirety of your existence, Heidegger suggests, is by regarding your death not as some distant but well-defined contingency, like being struck by lighting, but as an indefinite but impending certainty that is '*possible at any moment*'.[100] You do not live your life for a number of years and then stop, like an engine that keeps turning over till eventually it runs out of fuel. Every moment of your existence is affected by your death, or rather your 'being towards death'. You are essentially finite: your days are numbered. (People are sometimes praised for being 'generous with their time'; and perhaps there is no other kind of generosity: the idea of generosity would not make much sense if we were never going to die.) You may strive to forget it, but your life is always informed by your sense of its ending.

It is a commonplace that death is the great leveller; but in another way, as Heidegger points out, it is what 'individualizes' us most absolutely. Death does not endow us with 'individuality' in the sense of a distinctive inner personality, but it establishes the bare differences that separate one existence from another: the tombstone facts of life. Despite the thoroughgoing sociality of the 'with-world', every existence is, in the end, radically 'non-relational'. Your death concerns you uniquely, because when you die, your being-in-the-world-with-others comes to an end, but theirs, though it may be affected in one way or another, continues. The only sense in which you can grasp your existence as a whole is by confronting the 'possibility of no-longer-being-able-to-be-there' as your 'ownmost possibility', and thus seeing your life as a permanent incompleteness that will nevertheless come to an end.[101]

Of course, the common sense of our they-self will find all this philosophizing about death rather morbid and irritating. It will acknowledge the fact of death with a wave of the hand and 'an air of superiority', but it will avoid thinking about its implications.[102]

'Dying' is levelled off to an occurrence which reaches Dasein, to be sure, but belongs to no one in particular. Dying, which is essentially mine in such a way that no one can be my representative, is perverted into an event of public occurrence which the 'they' encounters ... This evasive concealment in the face of death dominates everydayness so stubbornly that, in being with one another, the 'neighbours' often still keep talking the 'dying person' into the belief that he will escape death and soon return to the tranquillized everydayness of the world of his concern. Such 'solicitude' is meant to 'console' him ... At bottom, however, this is a tranquillization not only for him who is 'dying' but just as much for those who 'console' him ... Indeed the dying of others is seen often enough as a social inconvenience, if not even a downright tactlessness, against which the public is to be guarded.[103]

'Everyone's got to die', we will say with a shrug and a comic-glum expression. But it is only the chatter of the they-self, trying as usual to distract us from the fact that we all have to die our own deaths, alone in our non-relational contingency.

No doubt common sense will suspect a conflict between the open involvement with the world to which we are summoned by our conscience, and the non-relational isolation that comes to light in our being-towards-death. But common sense misinterprets death and conscience just as it misinterprets everything else. Moreover – or so Heidegger will try to persuade us – all its misinterpretations, and hence all our inauthenticity, can be traced back to a single source: our commonsense understanding of time.

In the first place, time can be understood as 'world-time', the practical time of ready-to-hand equipment – of harvests and meals, trysts and tasks, of getting up and going to bed.[104] World-time is quite literally the time of 'everydayness', because, like everyday spatiality, it is defined for us by the rising and setting of the sun.

In its thrownness Dasein has been surrendered to the changes of day and night ... The 'then' with which Dasein concerns itself gets dated in terms of something which is connected with getting bright ... – the rising of the sun ... Concern makes use of the 'being-ready-to-hand' of the sun, which sheds forth light and warmth ...

In terms of this dating arises the 'most natural' measure of time – the day.[105]

Under the guidance of common sense, however, we contrive to misunderstand world-time. We uncouple it from the web of its involvements with the world, and link it to a 'now' conceived of as a fleeting instant that is momentarily present to us. We forget about the temporality of anticipation and memory, and reduce futurity to the 'not yet now – but later', and pastness to the 'no longer now – but earlier'.[106] We picture ourselves as leaning over the parapet of a bridge, staring down at a mighty river. Shrouded in mist, it sweeps towards us from its inscrutable sources in time future; we catch a glimpse of it for the brief instant when it passes beneath us as time present; and then it hurries out behind us into the unfathomable oceans of time past.

Taking our clue from this image of time 'as a succession, as a "flowing stream" of nows, as the "course of time"', we go on to treat it as if it were present-at-hand to us within-the-world – in short, as what Heidegger calls *now-time* – the objective, infinite, homogeneous time of the natural sciences.[107] We then project this conception of time back on to ourselves, and start to think of our lives as made up of self-sufficient 'now-points' (rather like the 'I-points' of the ordinary conception of selfhood). We come to regard a lifetime as a series of 'experiences', as separate from each other as the frames of a film-strip, each one 'present' to us for only a fleeting instant.

> The remarkable upshot is that, in this sequence of experiences, what is 'really' 'actual' is, in each case, just that experience which is present-at-hand 'in the current 'now'', while those experiences which have passed away or are only coming along, either are no longer or are not yet 'actual'. Dasein traverses the span of time granted to it between the two boundaries, and it does so in such a way that, in each case, it is 'actual' only in the 'now', and hops, as it were, through the sequence of

40

'nows' of its own 'time'. Thus it is said that Dasein is 'temporal'. In spite of the constant changing of these experiences, the self maintains itself throughout with a certain selfsameness.[108]

We may, of course, find some comfort in this conception of temporality: if our lives are strings of separate experiences then we can imagine them continuing for ever. But we must also be aware, if only obscurely, that it is inauthentic: ontologically, we know that to live our lives in terms of now-time is to be 'in flight' from finitude or 'looking away' from it. Living in the 'now', we transform ourselves into they-selves.

> The inauthentic temporality of inauthentic Dasein as it falls, must, as such a looking-away from finitude, fail to recognise authentic ... temporality in general. And if indeed the way in which Dasein is ordinarily understood is guided by the 'they', only so can the self-forgetful 'representation' of the 'infinity' of public time be strengthened. The 'they' never dies because it *cannot* die ... To the very end 'it always has more time.'[109]

But we all have an ontological conscience, and we can never delude ourselves entirely. Even in the dazzling noon of sunlit everydayness, our being-towards-death casts its shadow.

Common sense has made us think of time as an infinite river, and often we will wistfully implore it to slow down, or indignantly rebuke it for the ruthlessness with which it snatches away our brief moments of happiness and hurries them off to oblivion. If we were more consistent, however, we would be equally inclined to praise the rapidity with which the river of time is carrying our future joys towards us, and to thank the providence which constantly replenishes it and ensures that it never runs dry.

> Why do we say that time *passes away*, when we do not say with *just as much* emphasis that it arises? Yet with

41

> regard to the pure sequence of nows we have as much
> right to say one as the other. When Dasein talks of time's
> *passing away*, it understands, in the end, more of time
> than it wants to admit.[110]

Understanding more than we admit, we begin to be seized by an authentic understanding of time's finitude. Our ontological conscience warns us that the temporality of our existence cannot be authentically understood in terms of now-time. We do not 'exist as the sum of the momentary actualities of experiences which come along successively and disappear', but as entities whose every moment is already structured in terms of existing between birth and death.

> Dasein does not fill up a track or stretch 'of life' – one
> which is somehow present-at-hand – with the phases of
> its momentary actualities. It stretches *itself* along in such
> a way that its own being is constituted in advance as a
> stretching-along. The 'between' which relates to birth
> and death already lies *in the being* of Dasein ... It is by no
> means the case that Dasein 'is' actual in a point of time,
> and that, apart from this, it is 'surrounded' by the non-
> actuality of its birth and death. Understood existentially,
> birth is not ... something past in the sense of something
> no longer present-at-hand; and death is just as far from
> having the kind of being of something ... not yet
> present-at-hand but coming along ... Factical Dasein
> exists as born; and, as born, it is already dying, in the
> sense of being-towards-death. As long as Dasein facti-
> cally exists, both the 'ends' and their 'between' *are*, and
> they *are* in the only way possible on the basis of Dasein's
> being as *care* ... As care, Dasein *is* the 'between'.[111]

Authentic temporality belongs to us as much as we belong to it; it is not a force of nature so much as the way our existence 'temporalizes' itself and its world. It is not an infinite sequence of uniform self-contained now-points, but a finite structure of differentiated 'moments'.

The moments of authentic temporality are 'ecstatic' in the sense that they 'stand outside of themselves'. They are linked to each other by countless pathways of memory and anticipation: they are not positions fixed on a bridge over time, but indefinite fields that reach out into both past and future.[112] Moments are 'futural', but not in the sense of being oriented towards infinite times to come. Each moment is magnetized by finitude, anticipating death like a compass needle pointing to the North pole.

> By the term 'futural', we do not here have in view a now which has *not yet* become 'actual' ... [but] the coming in which Dasein, in its own most potentiality-for-being, comes towards itself ... Only so far as it is futural can Dasein *be* authentically as having been. The character of 'having been' arises, in a certain way, from the future ... and in such a way that the future which 'has been' (or better, which 'is in the process of having been') releases from itself the present. This phenomenon has the unity of a future which makes present in the process of having been; we designate it as *temporality*.[113]

Common sense and natural science may try to persuade us that this finite, qualitative temporality is merely an arbitrary, human-centred interpretation of the objective flow of infinite time, rather like the grid of colour-distinctions that we lay over the continuum of different wavelengths of light. But we know in our ontological conscience that the analogy is false. Light is a natural phenomenon within the world, and we may or may not understand it. Time is different: like truth, we need to have some grasp of it if we are to understand anything else at all. And if we did not already understand time authentically, in terms of the ecstatic moments of our finite existence, then we would never be able to construe 'the "time" which is accessible to the ordinary understanding' – the world-time of everyday common sense and the now-time of natural science.[114]

World-time and now-time arise when 'the ecstatical character of primordial temporality has been levelled off', and the
moments of our existence have been 'shorn' of their
relations to birth and death so that they can 'range
themselves along one after the other' and thus 'make up
the succession'.[115] Ordinary knowledge, in short, depends
on a misconstrual of authentic temporality; and we have no
understanding of the world that is not attended by
misunderstanding.

Science and History
If Heidegger is right, then our attempts to radicalize our
pre-ontological interpretations will have led us to a fairly
clear result: that (though he never expresses it so baldly) our
existence as Dasein consists in the ecstatic temporalization
of our finite temporality. Equipped with this conclusion, we
can now revisit the phenomena explored in Division One,
and instead of groping our way from the everyday world
towards an authentic selfhood that remains a foggy mystery to us, we can start from an ontological concept of
authentic temporality and work our way back to the
everyday phenomena that both express and conceal it. The
unsynthesizable movements of thrown projection, for
instance, or the totalizing ambitions of discourse and care,
will now be defined as various general forms of temporalization, while understanding is specifically aligned with
futurity, mood with the past, and falling with the
present.[116] Finally we can begin to understand why authentic temporality had to be 'levelled off' into world-time and
now-time in order for the world and the items that are
ready-to-hand and present-at-hand within it to become
accessible to us in everydayness and in science.[117]

At first sight, there appears to be a trade-off between
scientific enlightenment and existential authenticity: in
winning the world for science, it would seem, we lose our
selves to the world. The world of objective nature may have
been brought within the scope of our understandings; but

44

our understandings have been abandoned to the world, and they wander through it in such aimless bemusement that we can scarcely recognize them as our own.

But perhaps the dilemma is unreal. Maybe we can, as Heidegger suggests, develop an 'existential conception of science' that will enable us to recognize the sciences as Dasein's handiwork without diminishing their claim to objectivity. He begins with natural science, considered as 'the theoretical discovery of the present-at-hand'. It cannot, he points out, be defined in terms of theory as opposed to practice, since every theoretical inquiry involves 'a praxis of its own', from the construction of experimental apparatuses in physics, to the preparation of samples in biology, and techniques of writing and notation in more formal disciplines.[118] But what makes a theoretical practice scientific?

Heidegger's paradigm of a scientific theoretical practice was the kind of mathematical physics associated with Newton: for him it remained an unrivalled example of successful science, even though it had been thrown into crisis by Einstein.[119] Traditionally, there were two antithetical explanations for its success, one stressing Newton's attentiveness to the messy empirical facts of experience, the other emphasizing his determination to apply pure mathematical reasoning to them. Heidegger advises us to be suspicious of both interpretations:

What is decisive for its development does not lie in its rather high esteem for the observation of 'facts', nor in its 'application' of mathematics in determining the character of natural processes; it lies rather in *the way in which nature herself is mathematically projected* ... by looking at those constitutive items in it which are quantitatively determinable (motion, force, location, and time). Only 'in the light' of a nature which has been projected in this fashion can anything like a 'fact' be found and set up for an experiment regulated and delimited in terms of this projection. The 'grounding' of 'factual science' was possible only because the research-ers understood that in principle there are no 'bare facts'.[120]

The truths discovered by Newtonianism depend, in other words, not only on nature's regular habits, but also on the conjectures of those seventeenth-century investigators who chose to 'project' it in a way that brought themes like motion, force, time and location into focus and made them available for objective knowledge. The 'thematization' performed by scientific inquirers is not so much the effect of objectivity as its precondition:

> Its aim is to free the entities we encounter within-the-world, and to free them in such a way that they can 'throw themselves against' a pure discovering – that is, that they can become 'objects'. Thematizing objecti-fies.[121]

Different thematizations (Newtonian and Einsteinian for example) deliver different aspects of nature to scientific knowledge, and the choice of thematization depends on scientists rather than on nature itself. Scientific progress does not follow a path predetermined by nature itself: like all our activities, science always has an open future.

But what if the object of inquiry is ourselves, as entities whose existence consists in our temporalization of tempor-ality and hence in our interpretations and misinterpreta-tions of ourselves and our world? The clue, according to Heidegger, lies in the 'fundamental existential ontological assertion' that 'Dasein is historical'. If we are essentially temporalization, then we are essentially 'historicality' too. Only by understanding our historicality existentially, and making it our own, can we ever hope to construct a 'science' of history.[122]

On first hearing, this suggestion sounds similar to the traditional doctrine of 'historicism', according to which human affairs are 'essentially historical' and therefore not representable with that peculiar combination of universality and precision that characterizes the natural sciences. Historicism can be divided into two diametrically opposed forms. The first is associated with the historian Leopold von Ranke, and states that human events can be understood only in terms of their own specific place and time; the other, associated with the philosopher G. W. F. Hegel, insists that they cannot be grasped in their full significance unless they are set in the context of the overall progressive sweep of history as it moves towards its final goal. But the two kinds of historicism have a great deal in common, and both of them are very congenial to common sense. For we are all everyday historians in our own case, rather as we are all our own ontologists. We can scarcely exist without having some sense of history and our place in it – of the oddity of 'the past', the historically distinctive features of 'the present', and the dangers and opportunities of the 'coming age'.

But even if historicism in its various forms joins with existential analysis in trumpeting the theme of historicality, their interpretations of it are fundamentally opposed. From the existential point of view, historicism attributes a false objectivity to history: it not only forgets that the historian's existence is itself historical, but also insists on slicing the historical record into separate 'epochs', thus locking past existences inside closed temporal cells as if their significance were a matter for their age only. Just as scientism reduces temporality to the self-enclosed instants of 'now-time', so historicism reduces historicality to the sealed epochs of 'world-history'.[123]

Historicism adapts history to the tastes of our they-self, which is not only anxious to keep up to date and conform with the norms of its epoch, but also susceptible to the charms of anything quaint and old-fashioned. The they-self finds in historicism a mechanism for evading authentic historicality.

It cannot repeat what has been, but only retains and

receives the 'actual' that is left over, the world-historical that has been, the leavings, and the information about them that is present-at-hand ... Lost in the making present of the today, it understands the 'past' in terms of the 'present' ... When ... one's existence is inauthentically historical, it is loaded down with the legacy of a past which has become unrecognizable, and it seeks the modern.[124]

If Descartes offered the supreme philosophical expression of inauthentic spatiality, then Hegel performed the same service for inauthentic temporality. He interpreted history as the work of 'the negative', which required us to pass wearily from error to error, negating each one on our way, until eventually we would arrive at the single great truth that had always been awaiting us at the end. Hegelian progress, as Heidegger comments, occurs 'knowingly and knows itself in its goal'.[125] For Hegel, history would end in the fullness of time, when we finally achieved complete self-understanding through 'the tremendous power of the negative'.[126]

But our conscience ought to grow restive at this point, for we know very well that history is not a gale that blows us where it wishes, any more than temporality is a river that flows inexorably on. Time and history are not forces that act on our existence from outside, but its very substance: we exist in-the-world by temporalizing our ecstatic temporality and by 'historizing' our ecstatic historicality. Historizing always takes place in the midst of an endlessly irreconcilable strife between 'destiny' and 'fate' – between the unchosen circumstances into which our 'community' and 'generation' have been 'thrown', and the 'essentially futural' resoluteness with which we project our inheritance and make it, for the moment, our own.[127]

Historicism tries to extinguish the essential conflict between destiny and fate by reducing history to a mere chronicle of an inert past – an unfolding sequence of unambiguous realities that are now over and done with.

Authentic history, in contrast, is a constant struggle to keep past existences open to the future.[128] The motor of history, for Heidegger, is not the 'tremendous power of the negative' but the 'quiet force of the possible'.[129]

We must hope that this quiet force will be strong enough to sustain us through the tasks that Heidegger has planned for the remainder of *Being and Time*. We need to be prepared not only for the third division of Part One (which will 'seek a *way* of casting light on the fundamental question of ontology'), but also for the whole of Part Two (devoted to 'destroying [or 'deconstructing'] the history of philosophy' in three backward historical steps).[130] But perhaps we can already make out the path that Heidegger will want us to take: a path that keeps us away from both absolutism and relativism, and repeatedly brings us back, surprised, to our own finite existence as interpreters and misinterpreters of the world, as askers of the question of the meaning of being, and as ontologists who can at last see why history is truth's best friend.

CONCLUSION

But that is all. Part One lacks its third division, and the three divisions of Part Two are missing as well. Perhaps fittingly, Heidegger never completed his treatise on the impossibility of completion.

In one sense the purpose of the work was fully achieved, for in 1928 Heidegger secured the professorship at Freiburg that was to satisfy his academic ambitions for the rest of his life. Meanwhile *Being and Time: First Half* had become a vast public success, indeed a classic, and Heidegger soon gave up the dream of publishing a complete version. He went on writing for another 50 years – till his death in 1976 at the age of 86 – but his favoured forms, brilliantly used, would now be the essay and the lecture rather than the systematic treatise. There have been several attempts to 'reconstruct' the missing divisions from this later material, but Heidegger's frequent remarks about his enigmatic 'turn' from the problematics of *Being and Time* throw grave doubt on them all. The title's implicit promise of a second 'half' was dropped in 1953.

The easiest way of conferring a retrospective completion on *Being and Time* is by connecting its idea of the historicality of truth with the fact that from 1933 to 1945 Heidegger was a member of the Nazi party in Baden, and that he was then suspended from teaching for a period of 'denazification' which lasted six years. In 1948 he told Herbert Marcuse that he had originally expected Nazism to bring about 'a spiritual renewal of life in its entirety, a reconciliation of social antagonisms, and a deliverance of western existence from the dangers of Communism', but that it had not worked out as he hoped. He also quoted Jaspers: 'that we remain alive is our guilt'.

Alternatively, one might see *Being and Time* as seeking

completion in the work of others, including many who would be affronted by any association with 'Heideggerianism'. For instance, there are Levinas's invocations of the unassimilable 'other', Simone de Beauvoir's critiques of 'feminine' inauthenticity, Sartre's criticisms of traditional psychology and ethics, and Althusser's and Foucault's revolts against 'historicism' and 'humanism', not to mention Derrida's unmistakable Heideggerian programme of 'deconstruction'. Or there are the attempts by theologians such as Bonhoeffer, Buber, Bultmann and Tillich to 'demythologize' religious belief, Lacan's revolt against 'ego-psychology', or the 'humanistic' psychologies of Binswanger, Rogers and R. D. Laing. Then there is the vast tradition of 'western' or 'cultural' Marxism, carried forward by Lukács, Marcuse and Adorno; the various strands of 'interpretative' sociology from Schütz to Bourdieu; and the 'history from below' initiated by E. P. Thompson and Emmanuel Leroi Ladurie. Or there is Anglo-American 'philosophy of mind', rooted in the anti-Cartesianism of Gilbert Ryle, and the anti-positivistic theory of science pioneered by Alexandre Koyré and Thomas Kuhn. The greatest adventures of twentieth-century thought, in other words, may be little more than an incomplete series of footnotes to Heidegger's *Being and Time*.

NOTES

References give section number, followed by the page number of the German edition (H: *Sein und Zeit*, seventh edition, Max Niemeyer, Tübingen, 1953) and of the classic English translation (MR: *Being and Time*, translated by John Macquarrie and Edward Robinson, Blackwell, Oxford, 1962). All quotations are taken from this translation, with the permission of Basil Blackwell Ltd.

1. Epigraph, H1, MR19.
2. Epigraph, H1, MR19.
3. §32, H152, MR193.
4. Epigraph, H1, MR19.
5. §1, H2, MR21.
6. §1, H2, MR21.
7. §1, H3–4, MR22–3.
8. §1, H6, MR26.
9. §1, H4, MR23.
10. §2, H5, MR24.
11. §2, H5–6, MR25–6.
12. §7, H37, MR62.
13. §4, H12, MR32.
14. §4, H12, MR32.
15. §4, H15, MR35.
16. §4, H13, MR34.
17. §5, H15, MR36.
18. §5, H16, MR37.
19. §6, H25, MR47. ('Presence' and 'present' correspond to *Anwesenheit* and *Gegenwart* in the original.)
20. §6, H21, MR43.
21. §6, H20, MR41.
22. §5, H15, MR36, §6, H21, MR42.

23. §8, H39–40, MR63–4.
24. §9, H41, MR68; see also H41, MR65.
25. §9, H44, MR69.
26. §23, H109, MR144.
27. §15, H68, MR98.
28. §22, H103–4, MR137.
29. §23, H105–6, MR140.
30. §16, H73–4, 76; MR102–4, 107.
31. §21, H100, MR133; cf. §14, H65, MR94, §12, H59, MR86.
32. §15, H68, MR96–7.
33. §21, H100, MR133.
34. See §21, esp. H99–100, MR132–3.
35. §21, H96, MR129.
36. §21, H100, MR133.
37. §10, H46, MR72.
38. §25, H115, MR151.
39. §13, H62, MR89.
40. §26, H124, MR162.
41. §25, H115–16, MR151.
42. §25, H116, MR152.
43. §25, H117–18, MR153–4.
44. §26, H118, MR155; H124, MR161.
45. §26, H122, MR158–9.
46. §26, H118, MR155.
47. §26, H120, MR156–7.
48. §27, H127, MR164; H128, MR165–6.
49. §27, H127, MR165.
50. §27, H126, MR164.
51. §35, H168, MR212.
52. §36, H172–3, MR216–17.
53. §37, H173–4, MR217–19.
54. §38, H178, MR223.
55. H167, MR211; §38, H175–6, MR220.
56. §27, H127, MR164.
57. §29, H138, MR177.

58. §29, H136, MR175.
59. §29, H138, MR177.
60. §31, H145, MR185.
61. §31, H148, MR188.
62. §31, H144, MR184.
63. §32, H152–3, MR194–5; see also §63, H314–15, MR362–3.
64. §34, H164, MR208.
65. §38, H179, MR223; §44, H229, MR272.
66. §28, H133, MR171.
67. §41, H192, MR236.
68. §40, H186, MR231.
69. §40, H188–9, MR233.
70. §40, H188, MR233.
71. §44, H215, MR258.
72. §44, H228–9, MR271; §43, H202, MR246.
73. §43, H203, MR247.
74. §43, H204, MR248.
75. §43, H205, MR249.
76. §43, H202, MR246–7.
77. §43, H206, MR250.
78. §43, H206, MR249.
79. §44, H229, MR271.
80. §44, H214, MR257.
81. §44, H222, MR265.
82. §44, H225, MR268.
83. §44, H219, MR262.
84. §44, H220, MR262.
85. §44, H220, MR262.
86. §39, H183, MR228.
87. §21, H101, MR134.
88. §44, H226–7, MR269.
89. §34, H165, MR208.
90. §63, H315, MR363; H313, MR361.
91. §38, H179, MR224; see also §27, H130, MR168; §54, H267, 268, MR 312, 313.

92. §63, H315, MR363.
93. §55, H271, MR316.
94. §56, H273, MR318.
95. §58, H284, MR330.
96. §57, H274, MR319.
97. §48, H243, 242, MR287, 286.
98. §47, H238, MR282.
99. §48, H244, MR288.
100. §52, H258, MR302.
101. §50, H250–1, MR294–5.
102. §52, H258, MR302.
103. §51, H253–4, MR297–8.
104. §80, H414, 420, MR467, 472.
105. §80, H412–13, MR465–6; cf. §22, H103–4, MR137.
106. §65, H326–7, MR374–5; see also §61, H304, MR352.
107. §81, H421–2, MR474.
108. §72, H373, MR425.
109. §81, H424–5, MR477.
110. §81, H425, MR478.
111. §72, H374, MR426–7.
112. §65, H328–9, MR377.
113. §65, H325–6, MR373–4.
114. §65, H329, MR377.
115. §81, H422, MR474.
116. §68, esp. H346, 350, MR396–7, 401.
117. §81, H422–3, MR474–5.
118. §69, H356–8, MR408–9.
119. §3, H9–10, MR29–30.
120. §69, H362, MR414.
121. §69, H363, MR414.
122. §66, H332, MR381.
123. §78, H405, MR457; §75, H388–9, MR440–1.
124. §75, H391, MR443–4.
125. §82, H434, MR484–5.
126. 'die ungeheure Macht des Negativen', see G. W. F. Hegel,

Phenomenology of Spirit, translated by A. V. Miller, Oxford University Press, 1977, Preface, p. 19.

127. §74, H384–5, MR436–7.
128. §76, H397, MR449; H393, MR445.
129. 'die stille Kraft des Möglichen', §76, H394, MR446.
130. §83, H437, MR487; §75, H392, MR444.